The Scenic

Route to

Purpose

The Scenic Route to Purpose

Tavis C. Taylor

Published by EvyDani Books, LLC
Copyright © 2019 by Tavis C. Taylor

Tavis Taylor
Tavis@TavisTaylor.com

Edited by Windy Goodloe, Nzadi Amistad Editing & Writing Services

ISBN: 978-0-9989945-8-1

Printed in the United States of America

Disclaimer

This work depicts actual events in the life of the author as truthfully as recollection permits and/or can be verified by research. Occasionally, dialogue consistent with the character or nature of the person speaking has been supplemented. The names of individuals have been changed to respect their privacy.

Dedication

This book is dedicated to all of those who have been or are entangled in self-imposed chaos, who are in the right place to receive God's grace and love. – T.T.

Tavis C. Taylor

Table of Contents

Prologue

The cream-colored dilapidated walls of the jail cell were caving in like quicksand in the Sahara Desert. This cell was not like those black iron see-through bars featured on *The Andy Griffith Show* when Ernest T. Bass got arrested for the fiftieth time. This cell came equipped with an iron-cement door that was about twenty-inches thick, and when the door closed, the sound made me shudder at the thought that I may never see the other side of it again. The sound was menacing and tormenting.

Some of these doors were operated by the push of a button that was controlled in an entirely different part of the facility, while others were controlled and opened by really huge keys that were longer than my forearm. Either way, I was not going anywhere until they gave me permission to. The cell contained cameras, so I was watched closely for twenty-four hours per day like a lion in the jungle, studying its prey and waiting to move in for the kill.

There was this particular part of the jail called "the holding cell." This was where I was held while awaiting my fate, whether it was to get bonded out, get transferred to another jail, or to be taken down into general population with the other inmates, where I would be handed a blanket and a mattress. Did I say "mattress"? Actually, it wasn't a mattress. It was a combination of five yoga mats. They were the cheap ones they sell at variety stores.

The stench of this jail triggered a part of my life that I was all too familiar with. My past had been checkered, and even though my life is on track these days, it had not always been.

My brushes with the law started around the age of thirty. As I sat in the holding cell at the Walton County jail, confused, lonely, and totally done with trying to figure out my life, I asked myself so many questions. One of them was, How could this happen today of all days?

I had just left the DMV. I had just gotten my license after not having it for three years. It had been suspended because I had received a DUI. At that point, I hadn't made any more legal mistakes. I had been a good girl. So I sat there with thoughts roaming around in my head, and finally I prayed. With the belly of defeat and the white flag of surrender raised, I muttered, "God, I haven't done anything. I am tired. I have fought for years to unspin the web of chaos that I have so eloquently spun. I honestly didn't set out to get the end results that showed up today! Here we are, twelve years later, and the residue of my mistakes still lingers. The stench of doing wrong lingers. The conscious wrong that I did many years ago, 2001 to be exact, still has consequences. And so here I sit, with tears in my eyes and the taste of defeat fresh on the palate of my soul."

I prayed because, *this time*, I had not done anything to deserve this. See, this time, I had made up in my mind that I was going to put all the embarrassment and shame behind me. This time, I was going to move forward and walk in my calling. This time, I was determined to tell my story, in hopes that it would give someone the tenacity and will to want to live, in hopes that people would say, "If the grace of God can help her make it through all of that, that same grace can get me through."

This time, as I sat there, my defeated prayer continued and sounded something like this, "I don't think I can make it another day. I have served You. I have done what was right. I have told others of Your goodness, and here I am. I just made a vow to You that I would tell my story and participate in the prison ministry that I know You called me to. I will make my book, *Behind the Walls: Making It through a Tough Time*, available to inmates, jails, and prisons throughout the world. This is the book that You inspired me to write while I was flat on my back, incarcerated, and needing a word of encouragement. This is the book that You inspired me to write when I asked the question, "God, will You ever use my troubles for Your good?" Then, I said, "But if that is not what You want, I will become an atheist, I will throw the book away because, God, I am so tired. But if that is not so, if ministry is what You want me to do, then please do like You did Paul and Silas and get me out of here! I'll share it. I'll share that book from that place, in the way You showed me."

Three to five minutes later, the doors made a loud humming sound. This familiar sound meant that I was on my way to the next phase of the torturing maze of the penal system. I was intimately knowledgeable of this system. The sergeant at the jail, wearing her stiff tan and dark brown sheriff's uniform, walked in and said, "Ms. Taylor, let's go."

As I walked slowly to the door, I asked, "Are the state police here to pick me up?"

She replied, "No, we called Fulton County, and they told us to let you go." As we walked down the corridor to exit the holding cell, my mind raced with a million thoughts. I couldn't help but wonder why did they arrest me and why did they let me go so quickly. When the doors opened for freedom, the officer asked, "Do you need to use the phone?" At first, I said, "Sure." I needed to call someone to come and pick me up. And then it hit me, I was free, free to go. I could not run the risk of them telling me to come back or them saying they had made a mistake so I opted not to use the phone. When they let me go, I ran. I ran and I ran. I went to a lady's house who lived close by and asked for two things: a ride to my grandmother's house and to use her cell phone. While we were driving, I called my supervisor to let her know that I was free. My release happened so fast, that she screamed in the phone, "NO, T! GO BACK!" My freedom happened so fast, that she thought I had broken out of jail somehow.

I later found out that one of my friends from undergraduate had a sister who worked a Fulton County Jail. She was relieving a coworker for lunch and intercepted the call letting Fulton County know that I had been arrested and answered the warrant. She told them to let me go simply because she recognized my name and the work that I did in the community. She either thought it was a mistake or that I needed to be free to try to work out the perceived discrepancies in the arrest.

The purpose of this book is to tell my story in a way that allows you to understand the consequences of your actions and figure out how to jump off the boat of chaos. In addition, I hope my story provides moments of reflection and transparency for you, so you can heal and stop going around certain mountains and be honest with yourself. What situations have you found yourself in? How has your life been affected by your decisions? In this situation, how did you handle it? Have you forgiven yourself?

All I can tell you is that I have learned to count the miracles that happen along the way. And after you finish reading this part of my story, you, too, will learn to count the miracles along the way, especially if you are like me and life has taught you things because, perhaps, your life has taken you on the Scenic Route to Purpose.

Tavis C. Taylor

Family Matters

I was born and raised in Monroe, Georgia. Growing up, Monroe was somewhat racially and economically divided. My siblings and I were blessed to have my parents because we were among the minority of little brown children who were being raised by married parents. At the age of eight, our parents moved my three siblings and me from the inner city part of Monroe, located near the public housing apartments, to the rural area of Monroe, which we nicknamed "the country" because there was little to no activity or people our age. This was supposed to be a safe place for us. It was so rural that we lived on a bumpy road.

My parents' friends always joked that they were in love when they married. I honestly believed it, but of course, no marriage was perfect, and like normal, they had their set of issues. I remember the chatter and conversations growing up regarding their marriage and them having "all those children."

I have two sisters and one brother. My oldest sister and I are less than a year apart, so we grew up pretty close. My mother was pregnant with me when she went back for her six-weeks check-up after giving birth to my sister. My younger brother lived with us sometimes and with my grandmother at other times.

The dynamics of our household were interesting. My mother was young when she and my father married. She was seventeen, and my father was twenty-four. In the beginning, we were living in public housing and moved from there to another apartment. At some point, we moved to a two-bedroom apartment.

My mother had always been ambitious and had decided that we should move from the inner city. Back in the seventies, things were not as strict, so my mom was able to complete the paperwork in my father's name and get us a new home. This home came complete with five bedrooms and two bathrooms. Now, in the seventies, that was a pretty big deal. I remember hearing conversations where my grandmother and others talked about my mother very negatively. They would say, "She thinks she is this. She thinks she is that" simply because she decided that her children needed to be in a different environment.

My dad had always been pretty laid back. He had served in the United States National Guard during the Vietnam War era. After that, he worked at a local plant and retired from a Walmart Distribution

Center. It was interesting because he worked at the truck gate where he met and greeted hundreds of people. Some of these people still call him on holidays and give him well wishes. These are the type of people my father and grandfather are: loving, gentle, and full of laughter.

Violated

"Tavis! Tavis!" I heard my mother calling my name. When I turned the corner running as fast as I could, she was waiting for me in her 1979 royal blue Mercury. As I approached the car, she pulled the lever on the bottom of the driver's seat and leaned forward so that I could get into the car. "What were you all doing behind that building?"

I said, "Nothing. He was trying to get my tag."

For some reason, she believed me. But what she didn't know was that he had pulled me into him with his right hand and had his private part in his left hand. I gave in to him because I was used to this, and I couldn't have been more than seven years old. This activity had become normal for me with different men connected to my family. It began with my uncle, who is now deceased. Molestation became my identity. I remember thinking that I was born for this, that the God that I went to the Baptist church to hear about had created me to be a sexpot for men.

I am not quite sure when it all began, but I was young. By the age of eight, my parents had moved us out of the inner city to the suburbs of Monroe, Georgia. My first sexual experiences happened before I can even remember. The "sexual demon," as I like to call it, can be really cruel and mean. I have heard stories of women who felt guilty because they became aroused or even had an orgasm while being molested. After years of feeling guilty about the same thing, I realized two things: One, when your body is touched in a certain manner, it may or may not respond, and two, once you awaken Pandora's box of sex, it is hard for you to put it to rest.

My uncle (we will call him Jo-Jo), who is now deceased, was a person I knew and trusted. Heck, everybody trusted him, and I will never forget some of the encounters that we had. He lived with my grandmother, and my parents would take us over there for my grandmother and her children to babysit us. We spent a lot of time there, and I remember one incident that involved two boys from the neighborhood. I wonder where they are now. I heard that one of them ended up on drugs. I think that was the one that my uncle penetrated himself. My grandmother used to run a liquor house when we were growing up, and as children, we were sent to hang out in the carport while the adults stayed in the house and partied. Oftentimes, my parents were not with us. They were taking a much-needed break from my siblings and me.

I remember the little boys being on top of me while my uncle watched with a flashlight. This happened several times and became the norm. I will never forget when my uncle asked me to go across the street to pick apples with him. I can still see that scene. He pulled out his penis and made me stroke it until white stuff came out. I think I was eight or nine years old at that time. I had never seen anything like it, and he told me to swallow it. I spit it out and ran. I remember hearing him say, "If you ever tell, won't nobody believe your ugly ass. I am the only one who gives you any attention anyway." So I lived my life hearing those words and feeling the need to prove him wrong. At least, I thought I was because, by now, I had several boyfriends. Little did he know.

It wasn't until I studied my behavior and searched for some rationale that I actually noticed the reasoning behind all my actions. What I didn't know was that a child who was a victim of prolonged sexual abuse usually developed low self-esteem, a feeling of worthlessness, and an abnormal or distorted view of sex. The child can become withdrawn and distrustful of adults and can become suicidal. Honestly, I became that child.

Tavis C. Taylor

Question Mark

Growing up in a rural town was very interesting. I always had questions about everything that took place. I wanted to know it all. I believed that everything happened for a reason and that there was an explanation for it.

As a little girl, they called me "Question Mark" because I have always been full of questions and always felt there were answers as to why things happened. I even had an imaginary friend whose name was "Plug-us-to-be." I am not sure where that name came from, but Plug was my friend. We grew up attending a Baptist church off and on, and of course, I had a million questions there as well.

I can honestly say that I was misunderstood as a child. I was always in the gifted programs at school and was constantly told that I was different and unique. I never was a problem because I stayed to myself. During middle school and high school, I was very active in sports. I also found my identity in being smart and athletic.

During my middle school years and high school years, I experienced what we now call "bullying." There were two young ladies who truly made my life miserable. They would say things like, "She thinks she is white. She thinks she is better than us." In fact, I didn't know who I was. Back in those days, our classrooms were separated by how smart you were and what your grades were from the previous year. I was always in the "smart" classes, and sometimes, I would be the only brown girl in these classes. Therefore, my day-to-day friends were mostly Caucasian. That was simply how it was and the life I lived during that time.

Troubled Young Adult

By the time I was a senior in high school, I was really troubled. I didn't have the best relationship with my parents, and I annoyed the heck out of my siblings. I truly felt misunderstood, and I felt as if I did not belong. I was able to get a part-time job at a sports store, and eventually, the family who owned that store became a surrogate family to me. High school was a very depressing time for me, and I vowed that, once I graduated, I would never return to Monroe, Georgia. I honestly felt as if no one understood me, especially my family. I was such a peculiar child.

As a child, I thought about suicide a lot. I felt as if God hated me. I would hear, "God is going to use you." My thought would be, God who? The one who allowed me to be molested? The one who allowed me to be misunderstood? God who?

During my senior year in high school, I had had enough, and I didn't want to live anymore. That was when I attempted to take my own life. After all, I thought, What difference would it make anyway? I took a lot of pills that made me groggy. It truly scared me, so I told someone. They rushed me to the hospital where they treated me by pumping my stomach and making me drink charcoal. I wanted my life to be over. Needless to say, the Lord spared my life, and I am grateful. I can remember the doctor saying how "lucky" I was to be alive.

Tavis C. Taylor

Getting Men

I didn't understand the impact that being molested could have on a person. I never hid that I was molested. I went to counseling and would tell my story of being an overcomer. Throughout my early years, I always had several boyfriends. In kindergarten, I had four of them fighting over me. They had purchased gifts, and my mother drove me to each of their houses to take them back. By the time I was in high school, I'd started dating bad boys and drug dealers, and for me, I assumed that their occupations were barriers to me falling in love. It was never my goal to have children or get married; all I wanted to do was have fun. I never wanted to run the risk of having a daughter that I could not protect.

My senior year in high school was rough. I was dating two drug dealers and really didn't care about either one. The older one caught me cheating. He took me to a hotel and beat me. I knew, once I left that room, I would never go back. It was at this time that I became so depressed that I attempted suicide again. What I didn't know was that I hated life and all the people in it. I was a middle child and felt as if no one understood me. I didn't feel as if I had a purpose. My friends were white, so of course, I had an identity crisis because I am not white and cannot pass for white. God was nowhere to be found, and all I heard was, "God is going to get you for this. God is going to get you for that." I was totally confused and couldn't help but wonder, why is He going to get me and not the people who molested me? I didn't want any part of that God. I vowed to get the hell out of my hometown and never return.

In my freshman year of college, I became pregnant by a very popular guy on campus. Honestly, as I look back, I was kinda happy that I was pregnant because I vowed that I would not treat my child the way I had been treated. Then, it hit me, what if I had to move back to the town where all the pain was? Anyway, the guy who I was pregnant by did not want me to have the baby, so we hightailed it to Atlanta, and I had my first abortion in my freshman year in college.

I stayed at that particular school for another year, and when I finally moved to Atlanta, I stayed downtown, close to the then Braves Stadium, in Carter Hall. It was a hotel-turned-dorm for students at State University.

I was dating a really sweet guy that I had met at Fort Valley State University. He had been in the Marines and was still serving on the weekends. We were in love. Our relationship was pure, and it was a happy time for me. There were moments where I almost sabotaged the relationship because I simply did not believe that I was good enough for him. People loved us together, and it was magical for a while.

During that time, I started cheating with an older guy named Paul. Paul was great, but Paul was married. He truly was a sugar daddy. He took such good care of me and my friends. While I enjoyed his company, sex with him was a task. It was truly a "hurry up and get it over with" situation. He bought me nice things and made sure I was fed, and he made sure I had enough money to survive. Eventually, that dissipated, and I vowed to be faithful.

I ended up getting pregnant by Paul, and those demons from the past started talking. We discussed how we were not ready to have children and how the best thing to do was to have an abortion. He politely took me to a private practice and held my hand every step of the way. It was for the best, right? We were not ready, right? He had a baby with another girl around the time our baby would have been born. He explained how it simply happened because she was one of his cousins' roommates and he would drive them back to college from time to time. Needless to say, I didn't leave him immediately, so there I was holding on to a relationship with a man who had cheated and brought a baby into the relationship. In my brokenness, I stayed. In my depression, I stayed. In watching his little girl grow for a while, I stayed. I put myself through so much pain, and by watching her grow, it only made me think of the second abortion I'd had. We finally broke up, and I was FREE!

While I was attending a university in Georgia, I started dating drug dealers again. My motto was "ain't nobody gonna hurt me again." I would be in control and maintain control. It was so bad that, for years, I could only have sex if I was on top. I was operating in a sea of sexual dysfunction, and I was living my life to the fullest, or at least, I thought I was. I was young, fine, partying, and in pain. The pain was on the inside. There was a void and a sense of emptiness that would not go away.

I settled down with this one drug dealer. We will call him "Rock." Rock swooned me, partied with me and my girls, bought me nice things, gave me a daily lunch allowance, and always took me to my favorite seafood restaurant in Atlanta called Spondivits. I honestly think we ate there every day for six months.

I dated Rock, who was from the hood, while I was pursuing my bachelor's degree. Rock was fun, and he was a challenge, but he adored me. I was his prize, "a college girl," or at least, that was what he told his mom and friends on the phone when they called. We drank our

Coronas, Absolut Vodka, and smoked our pot. Yes, I was a heavy weed smoker.

Rock had exactly what I needed to have the best time of my life or so I thought. He provided the alcohol and the pot we smoked. My friends and I didn't have to pay for anything because he paid for it all. I'm not really sure where he got his money from, and at the time, I really didn't care. We hung out in the projects, and we partied hard.

One day, when he was picking me up from work in downtown Atlanta, he saw me talking to a guy. When I got into the car, he questioned me. I said something flippant, and he slapped me so hard that my head hit the passenger side window. He said I was cheating and that he would not stand for that. I was crying. My mind was racing. I couldn't believe that he'd hit me. What he didn't know, at that time, was that I was pregnant. Yep, pregnant again. What was I going to do? I later found out that beating women was his thing. I had to figure out how to get away from him. I had an abortion, and eventually, we broke up. Well, we didn't break up right away. As a matter of fact, there were several more fights and beatings that took place, especially after one of my close girlfriends told him that I had had an abortion.

After we broke up, I simply stopped dating for a while. After a two-year hiatus, I was casually dating another guy. When Rock found out, he came over to my house, dislocated my shoulder, raped me, and left. Now, the irony of it was that I only opened the door because I thought something must have been wrong. We were not seeing each other, and he was dating someone else. He told me I was "marked territory." Needless to say, eventually, we ceased all communication, which was truly for the best.

Tavis C. Taylor

How Did I Get Here?

I can honestly say that I did not expect to get the results that were being revealed on a daily basis. I was sure that it had nothing to do with the current situation, and I was aware that there must be a deeper root cause of something more.

I am not sure how it all began. Was it the molestation? The rape? Was it middle-child syndrome? Who knows?! What I do know was that in 2001, my life began to unravel, and in 2003, I would have a date with the decisions I had made. And let me be the first to tell you that most of the miracles that God performed in my life were miracles that I needed because of poor decision-making on my part. I can't and don't blame anyone but myself. These choices did not just affect me. They affected everyone that I was connected to. But I will say, I did not expect to get the end results in any of the stories that I will share as it pertains to my testimony. It is also my personal confirmation to you that God is real and that He loves us so much that, even in my chaos, there were miracles along my scenic route to purpose. It is my hope that my chaos that led me to Christ will give you the hope and strength to allow your chaos to lead you to Christ as well.

It wasn't until after I lived in years of confusion and doubt that I realized that, perhaps, there was something deeper involved in my decision making. See, at the time, I didn't know that "we wrestle not against flesh and blood, but against principalities, against powers, against the rulers of the darkness of this world, against spiritual wickedness in high places" (Ephesians 6:12).

All I knew was that I was making wrong choices, and as the Apostle Paul said, "I don't really understand myself, for I want to do what is right, but I don't do it. Instead, I do what I hate" (Romans 7:15). I was making choices that I was rapidly regretting. But I couldn't see what was going on.

Can you or someone you know relate to the process of doing things that were contrary to what you knew and believed? That was what happened to me.

Getting Caught

"Hello. This is Tavis," I said.

"Where is Tyler?" the caller asked on the other end of the phone. Tyler is my son, and he was three years old when all of this took place. He was born in July of 1998. I was pregnant with him while getting my master's degree in public administration. I remember reading my books to him while I was pregnant, and when he was tired, he would kick me for rest.

Finding out I was pregnant with Tyler brought such joy and healing to my life. Having him cancelled out the pain of my past abortions and failed pregnancies. There was a void that his birth filled when he was born.

"What do you mean?" I replied, confused. Everyone around me knew that Tyler was in daycare that time of day. "He is at school," I blurted out in disdain for being asked such an annoying question by someone who knew he was at school. Then, I heard her whispering on

28

the telephone. "I can't hear you. What are you saying?" I flippantly said to the caller.

"You need to go get Tyler. They are going to come and arrest you at four o'clock," the whispering, scared voice on the phone said.

I slammed the phone down, grabbed my purse, and ran down ten flights of stairs. I remember that day like it was yesterday, and I can still see the stairwell when I close my eyes. I can still see the barbed wire that covered the stairs that were there to protect people from falling or to stop anyone from jumping. I also remember jumping those flights of stairs so quickly that, until this day, I can't imagine how I made it down ten flights of stairs in such a short amount of time, and I ran to my car. My only goal was to get off the premises before anyone could stop me. I wanted to get to my son before they took me away for life, or at least, that's what I thought. In a panic, I drove to retrieve my three-year-old. My thoughts were all over the place: Oh, God, what have I done? My son needs me. I am all that he knows. They have found out. I was scared yet relieved. I knew they were investigating me because I'd had a dream about it. The wait was over, and this day marked the last day that I would no longer have to look over my shoulder or wonder if I would ever be caught. This was the end of one phase of paranoia and the beginning of another.

I didn't realize that, on this day, my entire life would change and nothing would ever be the same. Even the way I looked at trees would change. What I didn't understand at the time was that all the years I had played Robin Hood with someone else's money had finally come to an end. Robin Hood is a legendary heroic outlaw who robbed the rich and gave to the poor. I knew it was coming. I'd had dreams that it would end. There were times when I would wake up in the middle of the night in a cold sweat, knowing that, one day, this part of my life would be exposed. Have you ever anticipated an ending to something, whether it was a divorce you saw coming or a big break up? What about that gnawing feeling that you had about your job ending, only to find out that it was the Holy Spirit revealing your destiny or fate to you? So I ran to the daycare, picked up my son, and decided to drive. I called my friend Jane and told her what was going on, and she said, "Just come here." I rolled down my window and threw my phone out as I was crossing over the Hill Street bridge in Atlanta, Georgia. My mind was racing; my hands were sweaty, and I didn't know what they knew. As my life flashed before my very eyes, I was looking back in the rearview mirror at my three-year-old, thinking, He does not deserve this.

Oftentimes, we make decisions without realizing the consequences of our actions. We make decisions on a daily basis, and we never take into consideration who they're going to hurt and how they're going to impact them. Honestly, I never expected to get caught.

As a matter of fact, getting caught was never something that crossed my mind. But it happened, and I found myself standing flat-footed in the face of destiny, death, and demise. Can you think of a time when you made a decision that changed the trajectory of your entire life? How did it impact others in your space? How did you handle the situation?

That happened on a Friday, and I'm sure they were very disappointed to find out that I'd left. I can't recall the phone calls that I received about people looking for me, but I knew that I had to go again on Monday to face my biggest fear. I had to go in as if I had no clue that they were going to arrest me. Knowing what I knew gave me the ammunition I needed to prepare to go in and have my date with destiny. See, here is the thing. This was really major because, over the weekend, I'd contemplated not going back. I'd contemplated going to Mexico, jumping off a cliff, or taking myself out with a bullet to the brain. Suicidal thoughts ran rampant through my head over and over again. The voices grew louder and louder as the weekend began to end. As a matter of fact, that Saturday night, I grabbed my .45 and went drinking. I hung out with a few friends and enjoyed their laughter. What they didn't know was that I had picked the park in Monroe as the place where I was going to park and blow my brains out. Yes, I was planning to take the cowardly way out and kill myself.

But I remembered that three-year-old who loved me so dearly and who did not deserve to live without his mother. He gave me all the strength that I needed not to commit suicide that weekend.

I spent the weekend trying to strategize. I spoke to my dear friends whose houses I ran to when I got the call. They helped me find an attorney, and he said just go back and see what they have to say.

Monday came, and I remember wearing sweatpants and a shirt, something comfortable, because I didn't know if they were going to take me to jail that day or not. I didn't know what to expect. So I rapidly drove to another friend's house, and I talked to her dad. He gave me a shot of moonshine before I went in to face my fears.

When I arrived, the executive director at the time called me into her office, where an entourage of onlookers were waiting to watch the fate of my chaos play out right before their very eyes. I heard the whispers as I walked in, "She is going to prison." The taunting words of one employee were, "That is what she gets. She thought she was better than everybody else." The staff at the office informed me that they would be raiding my office.

I remember feeling embarrassed and overwhelmed. I was looking around, wondering if there was a mole planted somewhere. I wondered if they would tackle me in broad daylight. I wondered if there would be a hostile takeover with guns drawn. Of course, none of that happened. When I arrived at my office, the executive director's door was closed. I cannot remember if she called me in or if she told the front desk personnel to send me to her office. However, I went and knocked on her door. As I stood there, I imagined I would be bum-rushed into a room with guns drawn. I even imagined that they would slam me down to the ground while the camera crew on Fox News caught the incident on film. When I entered her office, there were four or five people in there as well, awaiting my arrival. The Georgia Bureau of Investigations officer was there, roaming the premises, acting nonchalant. There was a State University police officer in the room as well. He had his head down. I honestly think he did that out of sheer embarrassment, not on his part but on my part. We had laughed and joked together before. After all, I'd worked there for almost ten years.

They began to interrogate me, asking question after question. I looked around at the office that was once a safe place for me to be, where I had been free to utilize my effective administrative skills. It had now become a holding cell of sorts. It became the place where the web I had spun would start to unravel. The round, caramel wooden table was a table that I had convinced the previous director to order, but it was now a resting spot for the sweat that dripped from my clenched fingers. I don't remember the entire session, but I do remember that I felt so afraid. I wondered what they really knew and how much they knew. After their interrogation was complete, they informed me that I would be escorted off the property by the police officers.

Wait. So they are letting me leave today? I thought. I get to go see my son today. Did I hear them correctly?

We left that office and went to my personal office, so I could gather my belongings. As we entered my personal office, I saw the picture of my son that sat on my desk, and it caused my heart to pound with guilt and condemnation. Different staff members sashayed by the office to see me. They all knew that I would be escorted off the property. I opened the desk drawers while the police, office staff, and GBI watched. They asked questions periodically, and sometimes, I told them information. I was exhausted and wanted to get this over with. I asked if I could make a phone call, and they told me yes. I called my dear friend Jane who knew where I was and what was going on. Jane asked, "What do you need me to do?"

My response was, "Just breathe!"

All I wanted her to do was just breathe on the phone and be present. Sometimes, it is important to have people who, no matter what you have done, are in your corner. That was one of the worst days of my life (at the time). They looked through my files, took what they needed, interrogated me, and escorted me off the property. As I walked through the corridors of the building, I remember wanting to disappear. Shame and fear were my best friends on this day. They would eventually be the only friends that I had, at least, until regret joined in. However, it was in that moment that I was grateful to be free, at least for now. After I was free to go, I drove quickly to my son's daycare to pick him up and get to safety.

The Original Arrest

I will never forget the dreadful day that all my wondering and worrying came to an end. It had been years since I had heard anything regarding my case at the university. Those years were long, dark, and full of paranoid moments. I honestly thought this investigation would never come to an end or a resolution.

This happened in October of 2001, and I spent the next two years full of alcohol and confusion, driving around, watching my back, and slamming on my breaks when I saw a police officer. My attorney had not heard from the district attorney for over a year or more. I didn't know when the day would come that I would get the call. I spent that time in full paranoia.

Finding work during that time was interesting. I was able to go to school and become a poly-tech (a person who administers sleep studies). That was a great job until the owner of the company wanted me to sleep with him or take a pay cut. Yes, you heard me right. He tried to force to me have sex with him and made it very clear that, because of what I was facing, this was my best and only option. If I did not sleep with him, not only would he cut my pay, he would fire me as well. I was stuck between a rock and a hard place. I knew I needed a job. I knew what I was possibly facing, and I knew that I needed to take care of my son, who did not ask to be in this situation. I spoke to my friend, who I was living with at the time, and she and her husband agreed that I did not have to deal with that.

Can you imagine how liberating it felt to be able to take up for myself while facing a major court case? After he fired me, I still looked for transitional employment. After all, I wasn't a convicted felon, yet. I was able to work odd jobs here and there until the dreaded day came.

One summer afternoon, I was driving home after picking my son up from daycare. He was five years old at the time. As I drove down my parents' road, I passed a sheriff along the way. When he slammed on his brakes, I knew that my date with fate had arrived. I looked up, and I passed another sheriff's car, and my heart started palpitating. My mind was racing, and I immediately worried about my son because he didn't deserve to see his mom like that, whatever that would be. Should I run? What should I do? I wondered as I drove. I forged on.

When I pulled into my parents' yard, there were three more law enforcement cars there: the GBI, SU police, and the Walton County sheriff. I pulled in and rolled down the window. The fear melted away as my motherhood instinct, the need to protect my son, overpowered everything. I looked at the agent with a boldness of protection, forgetting what I had done.

Wanting to protect my son from watching a scene that would have been etched in his mind forever, I said these words softly, "My son is in this car and what we are going to do is get him out, take him in the house, and then I will go with you."

The agent said, "Okay."

But what I didn't realize was that my dad had already firmly explained to them how things would happen on his property. Needless to say, my son was allowed to go into the house to safety, to where my parents were. The State University officer allowed me to go into the house to tell my son I loved him and that I would be back. Then, I got a jacket and closed the door behind me. And then he said, "You are under arrest for theft by taking and conspiracy to defraud the state. Put your hands behind your back."

My adrenaline was flowing. My palms were sweating, and my mind was racing. I was being arrested for a crime. Even though I had earned my master's degree, I was a criminal. My life flashed before my eyes. How could this be? How did I get here?

I can still remember the look on the State University police officer's face. His caramel-colored forehead wrinkled with signs of distress. His eyes welled with tears as if he was feeling the pain of arresting a familiar face or even his own daughter. I knew him from work. He asked, "Do we have to put her in handcuffs?"

The GBI agent snarled, "Yes!"

He put me in handcuffs, opened the car door, and eased me in. The State University officer was talking to the GBI agent who opened the car door abruptly and leaned as close to my face as he legally could. He said to me, "We are going to get all of y'all. Where is…" And he started rattling off names. He, then, closed the door, and we headed from Monroe to Atlanta.

That was the longest drive that I have ever taken. I have been to Florida from Georgia, from North Carolina to Georgia, but that trip was long. My mind raced. I didn't know what to expect. Plus, I had to pee! I wondered if I would be beaten up if I wet my pants in the back of the police car, and honestly, I was just nervous and afraid. I had never been to jail before. The SU police officer was nice and drove me to the State University police precinct. They fingerprinted me there. They were really nice, and they did not keep me there long. The officer explained to me that the SU process was protocol, and I had to go there first because the crime actually took place in their jurisdiction. However, because it was a state crime and a felony, Fulton County jail was where I would be carted off to next. This was a complex process because this university had their own police department. Because the crime was committed in their jurisdiction, I had to be taken there first for processing. It was police protocol, and I had no choice but to comply.

After being fingerprinted and booked at SU, they loaded me up and took me to the Fulton County jail and booked me there. The Fulton County jail experience was an entirely different animal. I sat there, wondering what would happen to me next. What would happen to my son? I didn't know what evidence they had, and I didn't know what was going on. They never read me my rights at my parents' house. As a matter of fact, they never read me my rights at all that day, so I never knew what the charges were at that time. I would have to wait until a later time to find that out.

So there I sat, *Ms. Master's Degree, Ms. Sorority Girl, thinks she is all of that and a bag of chips.* I looked around at the stainless-steel toilet that was only hidden by part of a wall. I looked around, and I saw prostitutes, drug addicts, people with DUIs, meth addicts, and then there was me. But it didn't matter what I was and what they were. In that moment, we are all in the same place. Not one of us was better than the other. We were all inmates. I was not more important or different than them. I was scared yet relieved. I was horrified yet going with the flow. I no longer had to look over my back. Those two years of waiting had been horrific, but that part of the journey was over. This wait was over. The need to try to figure out what the police knew was over. They had all of their information, and they were ready to move forward with prosecuting me and about fourteen other individuals.

In less than twenty-four hours, I was out of jail, and things got crazier and crazier. One by one, everyone in my case was carted off to jail or turned themselves in. We all had to answer the initial warrant. Everyone was cooperating so amicably that the warrants could not be cut fast enough. I knew that bailing out of jail would mean that I would have a court date at some point.

My Day in Court

The time lapse between the initial arrest and the court date was a little foggy. But guess what. Yes, you guessed it. That dreaded day finally came — the day that I had to go to court.

I was working at a sports store owned by a friend when I received the call from my attorney's assistant, Samantha. She said, "Yes, and at that time, you will turn yourself in to serve five years in prison."

I said, "What?" It hit me like a ton of bricks. Then, I simply said, "Okay," and hung up the phone.

It was time to pay the cost for my wrongdoing. The time had come for me to walk down the green mile of life and face the criminal justice system for my discrepancies.

My dear friend told me to call them back and ask for a better deal. After several conversations, the assistant district attorney agreed and offered to meet with me in hopes of gaining information on who was the mastermind behind the crime and gaining more incriminating evidence against others. When that dreaded day came, we drove from Monroe to Atlanta to meet with her. Of course, I was coached on what I was supposed to say to her. Now, let me explain this to you. My attorney told me to go in and tell the assistant DA the entire truth. He was a Christian man who believed in the word of God. While he was talking to me, I was thinking, "Thou shalt not be a fool and go in there running my mouth."

Once we arrived, we walked into this office that had a great view of the city of Atlanta. I thought, there is an entire world out there, and I am about to miss it. I was never ready for what she was expecting me to do. The two names she said caused me to almost pee in my pants. I thought, "No, ma'am, I am not a snitch." But out of my mouth came my truth: "I don't know anything about them, and they didn't know anything that I was doing." My attorney and I argued sitting right there in her office. At one point, I said, "Do you want me to lie?"

After all, everything was on the table now. They had investigated thoroughly and come to the necessary conclusions they needed to prosecute me. My goal wasn't to bring everyone else down. My goal was to own up to my wrongdoings and suffer the consequences behind them.

Needless to say, my attorney was quite disappointed. However, the assistant district attorney kept her end of the bargain and offered me a reduced sentence. She informed us that she would submit our plea to the judge and would be in touch with my attorney regarding the next court date.

In that moment, it was as if time was speeding up at an accelerated rate. I had faced the music and was waiting on my fate to be determined by the assistant district attorney and a judge.

The drive back to Monroe and the preparation were very long. My attorney and I talked about his horses and how the time that I was given would not be long. He told me to go do my "little" time and come back home. I am assuming he thought it was that simple, but it was not that simple for me. However, I knew I would have to adjust.

We were off to court at the beginning of August of 2003. Upon arriving in the courtroom, I was so afraid. I knew for sure that trouble was something that was easy to get into and hard to get out of. When I looked around the courtroom, there I was indicted with fourteen other people. My parents were there. Some friends were there, and the guys that I worked for at the time were there, too. The judge called my name to come up, and I thought, How did it get this way? How did this happen? Please do not let this be on TV.

I looked around at all the people who were involved, and I felt so guilty because I had gotten them involved. I was considered the mastermind of this case, and I know, by now, you're probably asking, "What did she do?" There I stood, facing fourteen counts of theft by taking and conspiracy to defraud the state. Yes, there were fourteen other people involved in my case with me. How did I steal these funds? I added people to the payroll of a major institution who did not work there. For example, if you were my friend or someone I knew, you would go to the Human Resources Department and complete an entire hire packet. I would submit your hire sheet through our department, which was really easy for me to do because, as the business manager, that was my job anyway. I would complete hire forms for project managers, and I would submit a false form for someone I knew. I added people to the payroll who either underworked or simply did not work at all.

What I did was wrong, and I cannot emphasize that enough. But it wasn't just wrong because I was literally stealing; I literally ruined the lives of others. This scheme set people up for failure because there were some who would never make $50 per hour, but they started to live a life like they did.

As I dealt with my own personal guilt and as I dealt with what happened and what we were all facing, I prayed. This was when I realized the power of prayer, repentance, and forgiveness. Let me explain, there were two specific times that I prayed during this chaos. No, this was not the only time I prayed, but I remember these prayers specifically.

I was downstairs at my parents' house in my childhood room, crying out to God and apologizing for the 900th time. As I was laying on a burgundy throw rug that my mother had purchased, I felt an overwhelming urge to stop what I was doing, fall to my knees, and cry out to God. There was literally one white lint string on the rug, and I prayed, "Dear God, if there is anyone that must go to prison, just let it be me and no one else. I am so sorry, and I am responsible for getting all of these people involved."

The second time I prayed the exact same prayer, I was at my friend Jane's house. I was upstairs in the room that my son and I had been staying in. I was sitting on the brown carpet, weeping as Tyler slept. I prayed the same prayer and cried out to God. My prayer was, once again, that I would be the only person who served prison time. I know you may be asking why I prayed that particular prayer. Well, first of all, some of the other people I was indicted with told me that, during their interrogation, they were told that someone was definitely going to prison. They were told that this case would be used as an example for others. Now, I know that I could have prayed a different prayer, but that is a story for another book.

When the actual court day came around, I went to face the music. I rode with my mother and father to court. I remember looking around the courtroom, and as we stood, I can't remember exactly what I told the judge, but I think it was something like, "I'm so sorry. This was not what I intended to get. This was not what I set out to do. This just got bigger than I even expected," or something like that. I don't know exactly what I said, but what I do know was what she said to me.

The judge looked at me and growled, "You ought to be ashamed of yourself. You have a master's degree. You know right from wrong." She also told me that I should feel bad that people in her courtroom were crying and they didn't even know me. I looked around and saw that they were crying. People that I didn't know were crying and shaking their heads. However, my heart broke when I saw my father crying. I had broken his heart and disappointed him.

The judge looked at me again and said, "You ought to be ashamed, and you better be glad I don't go against what the DA recommends because I could give you more time than that." It was at that point that I knew that I needed to be grateful for whatever I got. Shortly after that, I was sentenced to ten years, to serve three years in state custody. My attorney had worked out that I could get my affairs in order. I was given approximately thirty days for that.

I accepted it, and I owned it. But what about the little brown boy who only knew his mother's love?

Doing Time

The ride home with my parents was a long ride. My dad broke the ice by saying, "I didn't realize there was that type of money floating around out there." He even compared me to Heidi Fleiss. We drove home, and I knew what was next. I had to tell my now five-year-old son that I would be leaving him.

Telling my son was easier than I thought it would be. My friend Christie, who was a kindergarten teacher, coached me through telling him. I explained to him why it was important to tell the truth and be honest. Then, I explained that his mother was going to prison.

The time I spent "getting my affairs" in order included signing my parental rights over to my mother. Her temporary custody lasted for years after I came home as well. I remember calling the lieutenant to ask him what I could bring, what I could and could not have. His last name was Taylor like mine, and I remember him saying, "You really should contact your lawyer because you have no idea what is about to take place in your life."

When the moment came for me to turn myself in, I was actually relieved. No more looking over my shoulder or wondering when things would happen. Please understand, this situation had been dragging on and on and on. The chaos that began in October 2001 finally came to an end in August 2003. My parents did not want to see me go in, so I kissed Tyler goodbye before he went off to bed the night before I turned myself in and headed to Atlanta. My youngest sister lived in a condo downtown, which was perfect for me. I stayed there overnight and surrendered to the authorities at the Fulton County courthouse the next day. Let me tell you, we partied so hard that night. It would be my last time drinking, partying, and having a good time. And partied we did. I remember wearing a white T-shirt and beige sweatpants because it would be warm when I went to jail. This was the same outfit I wore when I went in to be interrogated by the police at the university.

Oh, and there was a "let me have sex" type of situation that happened before I left. I chose the person wisely because I thought it would be great sex with no strings attached. After all, I was leaving for three years. Make a special note in your mind that I chose this person specifically because there would be no strings attached, and it really wouldn't matter. In my mind, I was going to a place where I would be beat up and Big Bertha would take my baloney sandwich.

As we partied all night, I drank and drank and drank. I even smoked some weed because, in my mind, I didn't have anything to lose. See, prior to all this happening, I was truly a good-time girl. If you wanted to party and have a good time, call Tavis! I call this time in my life "BC." It was "Before Christ." Yes, I was saved, but I wasn't trying to live for the Lord.

When the sun came up, I was ready to be escorted down the green mile of life, never to return. I know I sound dramatic and extra, but the only thing I knew about jail was what I'd seen on TV. I was thinking like most of you. In my mind, prison was this sex-crazed, animalistic place that housed people who were unfit to live in our society. Let me dispel that myth. It was not that.

My friends agreed to take me downtown to the Fulton County courthouse to have my fancy date with destiny. Prior to them dropping me off, my breakfast consisted of me drinking a bottle of Absolut Vodka. As they recall to this day, I told them that I did not want to be awake and that I did not want to face what was next. We partied so hard. We laughed. We cried. We were afraid, and we were doing all we knew to do prior to be walking the kiss of death.

We made it downtown, and I slung the car door open as Ms. North was trying to park it and jumped out of that moving car. They were planning to walk me in for a sappy ending; however, I jumped out of the car, drunk and belligerent, and ran into the building to get it over with. They tried to catch me by coming into the courthouse and frantically looking for me. The officer told them, "We have already taken her back, and it looks like she is going to sleep a mighty long time."

I stayed in the holding cell at the courthouse for hours. I remember hearing different women say, "She's drunk." One lady even took up for me and told them to leave me alone. I was in and out of consciousness because the vodka had done its job, and that was to keep me out of my mind until it wore off. I had to sit at the courthouse the entire day until the women had court. We sat in a cell that looked like a walk-in closet with steel benches. The toilet was stainless-steel with only a part of a wall separating the toilet and the rest of the room. There were women there who were on drugs, and they would use the toilet in that small room. The smell of drugs and feces penetrated our noses and our pores like incense going to heaven, except this smelled and felt like purgatory. After court was over, we were carted off like cattle from the Fulton County courthouse to the Fulton County jail on Rice Street. We were shackled one to another and told how to walk.

Some of us had on blue jumpsuits, but I was still wearing my sweatpants and white T-shirt. We were then loaded up in a van where we had to be quiet and ride. We were still shackled hand and hand together. I am sure this was so that we would not run away.

Upon arriving at the Fulton County jail, we were hauled into another holding cell. They took us in groups to this big room, where we had to strip down naked and take a shower. They sprayed us with some type of spray. One of the most humiliating parts was when they made each of us squat down to the ground, spread our butt cheeks, and cough. This was to make sure we did not have any weapons or drugs stuck up our butts. After that, they carted us off to our pod. This was a huge room with iron bunk beds. Did I mention that they gave us a mattress a little thicker than a yoga mat and some other items? Because of my drunken state, I was ready to lay down.

I remember feeling free. I remember thinking that it was over and that I could finally put the chaos that I had created behind me.

My first night in jail was one of the first nights that I had slept in years. The chaos had come to an end. Or shall I say that a portion of the chaos in my life had come to an end because, little did I know, that the chaos was just the beginning.

So, while I was at the Fulton County jail, I made a commitment to take the lemons that I had picked and make lemonade out of them.

Tavis C. Taylor

I stayed at the Fulton County jail for five months prior to going to the Metro State prison to finish my time. While I was there, I noticed one of the inmates was reading chapters from Rick Warren's book, *The Purpose Driven Life*. That was a sign from God that I would be okay because that was the book I had been reading prior to surrendering to the authorities. I inquired about obtaining copies, and a counselor from the jail called me out of my cell one day to talk.

This counselor's name was Sydney Watson, and he explained to me that he was over a program called New Beginnings. He proceeded to tell me all about this great program. My response was, "Thanks, but no thanks." All I wanted him to do was simply give me chapters of the book, so I could continue my reading. He eventually convinced me to join the group, and that was one of the best decisions I had made in a long time. The New Beginnings program was a program that allowed inmates to participate in classes from nine to five. This program prevented us from sleeping all day and being lazy. The classes were taught by counselors, volunteers, and inmates. These classes included spirituality, GED, parenting, anger management, writing and even more.

After I got over myself and realized that my master's degree did not matter there, I joined the program. The program had a leadership team that consisted of inmates. Guess which position I was nominated for and held? You guessed it. Spiritual Advisor. My role was to pray and lead morning devotion. Each morning, before we started, we had a small church service.

While at the Fulton County jail, I learned to appreciate the gift of being a child of God and of favor. Every step of the way, God would send me a nod, a wink, or a miracle. At that time, there was a computer lab, and I was able to access it. The officer would transport us from one side of the jail to another side, via a car. There were only two women in the entire jail who had this access while I was there. It was me and Mrs. Jackson. I praised God for the mornings that we were afforded the opportunity to have coffee and real cream. They even gave us special treats sometimes. This included special food and simply treating us like normal human beings. The irony of it was that some of them would say they were never caught or had been one mistake away from being where we were.

One morning, the deputy decided to let us walk back, and I remember how sensitive I was to the air, the wind, the trees, and the road. As we walked, I was able to enjoy the sun. I was so grateful for the favor that was on my life. My attitude changed greatly when I went to the law library and researched the crime that I had committed and the time that I was sentenced to serve in custody. This day was a humbling day because I realized, in that moment, that the time and title of my charges that were handed down by the assistant district attorney could have been much worse. Honestly, I could still be in prison today for what I did in 2001.

From that day on, I served my time with a humble attitude, and I praised God the entire time. I made peace with several things. First, it could have been worse because the time that I was given could have been much longer. Second, I realized that the longest they could keep me was three years. My sentence was ten years, and I had to serve three years in custody. I learned, while I was there, that because I had never been in trouble before, I would only have to serve one-third of my time. Lastly, I knew that there would be life after this time. I knew that, at some point, I would be home with my son, and this would be over.

While I was away, I did my best to remain an active parent. This could not have happened without my parents. My mother accepted my calls every day and allowed me to talk to my son. My parents took really good care of him while I was away.

During my stay at the jail, my family and friends would routinely call the counselors, and I got into trouble for that. They simply wanted to check and make sure I was okay. After all, most of them didn't have any experience with jail life. All they knew was that I was in jail, and according to what they had seen on television, they assumed I was either being raped or beat up, so they would call. Well, this was not good because the counselors had other things to do besides tell my family I was okay every day. I will never forget when one of the counselors fussed at me, saying, "Tell your family to stop calling this jail! You are all right! You committed a crime, and you are in jail. You are not in college anymore."

Fulton County jail was a dark, dark place. I will share a few stories from there, and then we will move on.

Prior to going to jail, I worked at a sports store. One day, I received what was known as a special visit. This happened twice. The first visit was from two of the owners of the sports store. Can you imagine my face when I arrived at the visiting station and saw two Caucasian males looking through the glass? They had come to ask my opinion about something that was going on in the store with another owner. That may not be a big deal for you, but for me, it was. I was in a dark place, where society deemed me worthless, and here these guys were, free and home with their families, and they needed me. That was a sign for me that God can and will use people even in their chaos. The second visit was from a friend who was thinking of divorcing her husband. Now, can you imagine my face when I saw her standing there as well?

Honestly, being incarcerated validated the power in prayer and the prayer of agreement. One night, we prayed so hard that the sewer spilled over. The raw feces was coming out of the floors, and by the time they evacuated us and took us to another pod, the muddy liquid was up to our knees. I'm not sure what caused it, but I do remember saying, "God, I didn't sign up for this."

During my stay there, the guards would come and get me out of my room and ask me, "How did you do what you did?" The crazy part about it was that my crime came with a badge of honor in jail and in prison.

In January of 2004, I was transported from the Fulton County jail to the Metro State prison to go through the diagnostics part of going to prison. Diagnostics was where I was tested for everything under the sun. They gave me a physical test, a psychological test, and a written test. After I completed those weeks of testing, I was sent to prison to serve my time. All I could think about was not wanting to leave Atlanta. I knew, if I stayed in Atlanta, I would have the opportunity to see Tyler. That was my main goal. Therefore, I wrote a letter to the warden asking her if I could stay at that particular facility. I explained to her how I was sorry for my crime and how I needed to stay in Atlanta to be close to my son.

That was when the favor of God showed up in the middle of my chaos again. The warden came to the building I was in and summoned me out of my room. She had her team take me to the administrative building. My heart was racing because this was not the norm for where I was. Her bodyguard unlocked the door to one of the meeting rooms upon her request, and she ushered me into the room. Her security guard wanted to come in; however, she told them no and closed the door. She pulled up right there close to me and asked me several questions. She wanted to know what I had done, how, and why. She was actually impressed with the way I had written the letter.

I explained to her who I was and what I had done. I was one of those inmates that everybody wanted to ask, "How did you do what you did?" Of course, I explained to her what I'd done. She saw the remorse, so she allowed me to stay in Atlanta so that I could continue being an active mom. That was another miracle along the way on the scenic route to purpose. I forgot to mention that I did get in trouble for writing to her directly because, according to the assistant warden, I did not follow the chain of command, and he didn't know how the letter missed his hands in the first place. I apologized and silently thanked God for His angels taking the letter where it needed to go.

I spent the rest of my time there in Atlanta. Prison was nothing like television. I didn't see anyone get murdered, and there were no sex rings or orgies going on, but it was a horrible place to be, so I don't wish it on anyone. There were six of us in one room. Imagine having to share a room with six people, and in that room, there was only one sink and one toilet, and both of them were out in the open for all to see.

The favor of God continued to follow me the entire time I was there. I will share a few of the miracles that happened.

When I was in prison, I had to work at what's known as a detail. A detail is the free world's definition of a job. My one and only job was in the children's center. People wanted to know how I got that job. The other inmates asked who I knew and what had I done. I told them I knew Jesus, and I wasn't being funny or sarcastic. It was literally the hand of God. There were five of us who worked on this detail. The other women had spent a minimum of five years in prison. I came in and was immediately given a job in the children's center with them. The children's center was the place where certain inmates were able to have visits with their children. We cooked, read books, and played with our children. This was where my son would come and visit me. My parents would bring him to every visit like clockwork.

In addition to the children's center favor, the warden herself would utilize my skills for some of the things that she needed. I worked at the children's center until I was released. They had discussed allowing me to teach Microsoft Office to the staff, along with another staff member. However, this was shut down when the staff member told her it was not a good idea and that I should no longer have access to a computer because I might plan my escape. My point was, I didn't even have enough time to try to escape.

I was also a part of several prayer groups while I was there. It was amazing that I lived two truths at the same time. In the free world, I was the girl that was in prison for stealing money. In prison, I was celebrated for taking the money and respected for my ability to pray. The honor was there, and people would ask me to pray all the time. I didn't have to put on airs or dumb down myself while I was incarcerated. There was no competition, so I was actually free to be me in a place where so many people were shunned. I was physically incarcerated, but mentally, I was free, or at least, I thought I was.

Tavis C. Taylor

A Fresh Start

The time I spent in prison was a dark time. Even though I made the most of it, it took a toll on my mind and my body. I was ready to go home and possibly start my life over. I knew life would be hard and that I had been marked for life, but I was ready to face that. Things started happening and people started being mean and treacherous in prison, or perhaps, I was tired and simply ready to go home.

The day came when I could finally go home. I was free to go, but I wasn't really free because I was on probation and parole. This hit home for me when my parole officer came to see me one day.

I said, "It just feels good to be free."

She said, "No, Miss Taylor, you're actually not free. You still have one foot in the door." That was a reality check for me.

My actions in 2001 followed me for the next few years of my life. After all, who wanted to hire someone who had manipulated an entire system or be bothered with someone who had been in prison? Yes, I was free but not really free.

The stigma of prison stinks in the nostrils of many. There are even people today who will say, "You don't want to work with her. She's been to prison." I am okay with it because it is my truth. However, I honestly wasn't ready for what would transpire over the next few years.

Finding Work

Finding employment after leaving prison was quite hard. Now, before you say, "But there are programs for ex-offenders," please know that I tried all of them that were listed at the time. A lot of those lists were incorrect and were made up by someone who only God knows. Before leaving prison, I received a visit from a representative for the Georgia Department of Labor. I had written a letter to them regarding how awesome and timely the program they had at the prison was.

The commissioner at the time was Michael Thurmond, and he sent word to tell me that he would make sure I had a job when I came home. He was all for re-entry and helping those who were being released. This made me excited because, in my mind, I would be given a chance immediately upon my release. Unfortunately, that entire situation was an epic fail. The person he put in charge of it never found anything for me and made tons of excuses. He even offered me a chance to go out of town with him to work on a project that was connected to his personal non-profit. Of course, I was hurt behind that, and I did not go. My faith in the system started to wane. If the commissioner could not hold up his end of the bargain, where was I to get hope from? All of this caused me to turn to God even more. I wanted to know who God was and why I, in my opinion, could not seem to catch a break. The irony of it was one of my close friends told me it didn't work out enough because I wasn't humble. Now, the irony about that statement was that people constantly felt the need to tell me just that. My question was, "What does that look like?" I had nothing, and I was living with my parents. When all the chaos ensued, I had left my belongings at a friend's house. When I came home and wanted something or anything, she told me that her barn had flooded, and she had thrown it all away. All of Tyler's baby pictures, my degree, my pots and pans (those were special), everything was gone. Side bar: What she didn't know was that I went to see her niece one day, and my bed and pots and pans were there. Deep sigh. I, also, didn't have a car because it was a leased car and was returned a few weeks after I turned myself in.

I simply just wanted a chance to get my life back in order. I attended re-entry meetings and events in hopes that some program somewhere would give me a chance. I was invited to the table, but the tables never benefitted me, at least, not financially anyway. I would always hear, "Keep the faith. You're going to find something one day." "You are sowing seeds, and God will bless your sowing." The frustrating part about that was I was jobless, trying to get back into the workforce, and we all know, that made no sense. So eventually, I stopped. However, I continued ministering to the women at the Fulton County jail, and I still do that to this day.

Eventually, I was able to obtain employment from a friend who owned a convenience store. I was so happy to be free that working at the store gave me a peace of mind.

I worked part-time at the convenience store, and that was all right with me. Do you remember the guy that I told you that I slept with as my farewell sex? He started snooping around the store where I worked. The store owner and I had dated previously, and he didn't want the guy around. But that did not stop the guy, who we will call "Rico Suave," from snooping around. What I didn't know was that his ultimate goal was to conquer and devour all that I ever knew.

Drunk in Love

Honestly, I can't blame all that happened in my relationship with Rico Suave on him. I was looking for a sense of normalcy, so I thought, Maybe if I fall in love, my life will take on a form of normalcy. I just wanted it to be different, so in between "Falling in Love with a Stripper" (pun intended), I started a nonprofit organization with one of my best friends, Tanya Harrison. The nonprofit, Dreamgirls: Every Single Mother Deserves a Second Chance, provided resources and support for single mothers who were trying to change their lives. We were located inside of a public housing community where we provided life skills, a GED program, housing assistance, and mentoring. The project was not funded as promised, so eventually, we had to shut this program down.

During my time working at the store and Dreamgirls, Mr. Rico Suave would come and visit. He would make me think he was so excited and interested in what I was doing. In hindsight, I truly think he was, but our relationship was the perfect example of what two dysfunctional, unhealed people trying to mesh looked like. Besides, my job was to pray for him, not sleep with him. Needless to say, he pursued me like no other. What I would later find out was that his ultimate goal was to get me pregnant. He desperately wanted me to have his child. I know that sounds crazy, but that was what he wanted.

At the time we started dating, he was living with another woman. I did exactly what I said I would never do — I dated a man who was already in a relationship. Yes, and please note, that was a seed of karma I sowed that you will soon read came back full harvest. He eventually left her and continued dating me, along with his other football team of women that he had.

The conversation was great, and I was desperate for normalcy. I talked to my dad about it, and he said, "At least, he has never been to prison." So he said that I should give him a chance. His conversation was smoother than Smokey Robinson's hair and Idris Elba's smile. He won me over, and I fell head over heels in love with him. I loved everything about him: His walk, his talk, his smile, his conversation. As a matter of fact, because of the spirit of manipulation that oozed from his pores and the brokenness that I'd walked into, I limit my conversation with him now.

The conversation was amazing. He was charming and possibly my knight in shining armor. In our conversation, we talked about everything. We talked about children, marriage, etc. We dated for a while and decided to move in with each other so that we could be together.

It's Complicated

Did I mention that I was a minister of the gospel, operating in full disobedience, when I moved in with him?

I was so in love with love that I didn't care what it cost me to get it. I wanted love, a family, and my life back. I wanted what I wanted, and I figured that God was not moving fast enough at changing my situation, so I decided to get pregnant. Yes, we had talked and had decided that having a baby would be great. He felt he needed something for stability, and I was in love with love, so it seemed right.

We were dating, and I was falling deeper in love with him. I was ignoring all the signs of self-destruction. It wasn't all his fault. I accept full responsibility for the role I played in our chaos.

I was living in a beautiful log cabin in the middle of the woods, and he would come and visit. What he later told me was that he would read the newspaper before he came to visit so that we could discuss current issues. During this phase of dating, we were discussing having a child. I was so in love that I, the lady who had decided she would NEVER have another child by anybody unless their great-grandmother and entire family was going to support us, did exactly that. I was already a single mother, and I didn't want to raise another child on my own.

I remember the day that I told him I was pregnant. My friend Deotha went with me to get a pregnancy test from CVS, and I took the test in the store's bathroom. I was so happy. I knew I was going to have my king, my oldest son, and my new baby. It was so slickly planned that I created a vision board with the names of the baby on the board.

One day, we were laying in bed talking, discussing our baby. I was so careful when I talked to him that day. I asked questions like, "Are you going to take him to get a haircut if it is a boy?" "Am I going to have to chase you down for Pampers and milk?" "Are you going to keep the child?" Of course, all the answers were in favor of me having a child.

The first pregnancy ended in a miscarriage, and I was so devastated. I didn't know what to do. My dreams of being Mrs. Smith were ruined. My opportunity to have a family was over. After all, who would want an ex-offender? But the church girl and bad boy continued to date. My main goal at that time was to have a baby, his baby, by any means necessary. I started researching what I needed to do, and I did it. I took extra folic acid so that I could get pregnant. Two months later, I was pregnant again only to have this pregnancy end in miscarriage as well. Now you would think God was trying to tell me something, but of course, I did not listen.

This relationship was toxic on both of our ends. I needed healing and deliverance, and so did he. But we continued to date. He was my kryptonite, and I had to have him by any means necessary. After all, he was telling me how much he loved me, and I was crazy enough to believe it. Oh, and yes, he continued to date other women. One day, we were at his grandmother's house, and his little cousin walked in and said, "John got two durlfriends." (He was so young; he couldn't pronounce the word *girlfriends*.) I knew the kid was right, but John wasn't married, so to me, he was fair game.

That conversation stuck with me, and I was determined to stay in the race of winning the prize of "a black man who did not have any children and had never been to jail or prison." I know it sounds crazy now, but that was my truth as an ex-offender.

One night, I was so desperate for him that I went out on a date with a guy trying to shake this guy, and it went well. However, after drinking, I wanted him. I was yearning for my kryptonite. I decided to drive from Atlanta to Bethlehem, Georgia, to be with my boo. I took the country back roads because I knew I had been drinking. While on the back roads, I decided to stop and pee on the side of the road. Don't judge me. I had been drinking, and I had to use the bathroom. I was talking to him on the telephone and told him I would call him back. As I was getting in the car, I saw car lights come around the curve. There was only one car the entire stop! I waited at the back of my little burgundy Vibe for the one little car to pass by, but the car stopped in the middle of the road. It scared me because I immediately thought I was going to be kidnapped and taken away forever, never to return. However, the person got out and asked me if I was okay. It was a Walton County officer! I didn't need to get arrested because I was still on probation. He asked me if I had been drinking, and I said yes. I refused to blow into the blow machine, so I was carted off to jail. As I sobered up, I realized that I had really messed up.

I honestly didn't think I would be released because I was on probation. Typically, especially in Walton County and because I was on probation, I did not think I would get out of jail until my probation officer released me. Needless to say, the favor of God was with me because there was no hold, and I was free to go. I called my family, and my parents bailed me out of jail.

I felt like such a failure. There I was, arrested again and bringing shame on my family again. Not to mention, I would have to report my arrest to my probation officer. How would I face this? I didn't want to do prison time again. Here I was making mistake after mistake and not knowing what to do. I will say, all I could do was pray that God would be with me and grant me favor.

That next business day, I went to face my probation officer to tell her about my arrest. To my surprise, she complimented my progress and told me she saw so much in me. She told me that she was simply going to recommend that I remain on probation with the state. I breathed a sigh of relief and cried when I left.

Even though I faced that, I would still have to go before a judge in Walton County, regarding the DUI. With the help of my attorney, who is now a judge, I was given probation and a fine. Yes, now I was on two probations and responsible for two fines.

Shacking in Sin

My life continued to be a ball of craziness. However, I won temporary custody of the relationship with the guy, and we moved in together.

As a minister of the gospel, I didn't care. I just wanted that man, my family, a job, and to put my past behind me. Now, for some sick reason, I thought this was the way. I was like many single people who feel they can play God. I was going to make this relationship work.

Everything went okay for a while. We attended church together, and I sat in the very back of the church. I honestly thought I would get struck by lightning if I sat anywhere near a pulpit. Therefore, I didn't minister or participate in church activities outside of attendance.

After the second miscarriage, we decided to try again for a baby. This time, we went to the doctor to see why I'd had the two other miscarriages. I honestly was treating this situation like I was getting pregnant by a Rockefeller or a Kennedy and not a little brown boy from the hood.

The doctor performed extensive tests on me and concluded that it was not me. I used to joke with him that it was his retarded sperm. After all, he was the one who didn't have any kids. Needless to say, this time, we both took vitamins.

Y'all, it worked, and I ended up pregnant again. Once I found out I was pregnant, the doctor prescribed Prometrium, a medicine that was supposed to prevent miscarriages. We were so excited. At least, in each other's faces, we were excited. After all, we'd planned it! Then, it happened. You know, the cheating thing. When I was five months pregnant, he told me that he really did not want to be a dad.

Oh, I was pissed off, but I decided to give him what he wanted. I created some fake abortion papers and left them on the dresser of our bedroom. He was seemingly devastated and crying. I let the stench of mind games linger for a few hours. Then, I told him they were fake and that a pregnancy was not something to be played with.

We made it through the pregnancy with me making an inner vow that I could not deal with a known cheater. I would be leaving after giving birth to our son. As a matter of fact, I left during my pregnancy, and my dad told me to go back. He said, "He got you pregnant, so he needs to be a man." He was a cheating man, but he was still a man. Well, duh, he came in as a cheater.

When our son was three months old, I received a call from my mother. She said, "Baby, you don't have to live any type of way. I have money to help you move if you want to."

Now, how did my mother know that I was miserable and depressed? I have no idea. They say mothers know best. I remember praying to God, asking Him to get me out of this situation. I repented for operating in full disobedience to what God had called me to do. I had decided to move in with a man, unmarried, and have a baby. It was not the will of God, and honestly at the time, I was so broken that I dismissed it. But my mother knew, and she came to my rescue.

A few days later, we found a place for me to stay, and I let him know I was leaving.

Moving day finally arrived, and he was shocked. Now, his conversation to me was that he couldn't believe I was leaving, that no one had ever left him because he always did the leaving. His family members helped me move, and one of his cousins constantly picked at him on that day. One day, when he came over to see our son, he said, "This looks a little too much like home."

I said, "It is home!"

Tavis C. Taylor

Honestly, I don't think he cared one way or the other. I was out of his hair, and he could continue his gigolo ways. We continued to co-parent and had relations periodically. He was playing both ends to the middle. He was telling me he was allowing God to change him so that he could have his family back while being the bachelor that he enjoyed being.

There were simple things that bothered me. For example, when our son was three months old, he was sleeping in the bed with him and other women. One weekend, I almost lost my mind. I was going through postpartum depression that went unchecked, and I contemplated just taking him out. How could someone be so ruthless? I thought.

In July of 2010, our son was six months old. We argued constantly. I was begging him to buy Pampers, pay the daycare, etc. This whole act of deliberate disobedience had cost me so much.

One day, I was so angry with the mind games that he was playing that I went to a dear friend's house late at night and asked her to borrow some Clorox. I went into his house and put Clorox on every outfit he had ever worn.

Another time, I gathered myself and my children and went to his house because I felt he had another woman in "our" bed. At least, that was what he called it. Remember, we were working on getting back together, or at least, that was what I was being led to believe.

After several embarrassing moments, I decided to drop our son off with him and just go to Atlanta for the weekend. I disappeared because I did not want to lose my mind. On the way back from Atlanta, on Superbowl weekend, we were arguing on the phone. I was cursing so bad, and I was so angry as I drove past the Huddle House in Snellville, Georgia. Everyone knows that spot is a speed trap for the police, and I was definitely speeding through there while cursing him out. Guess what happened! Yes, I received my second DUI while talking to him on the phone! When I received the first DUI, I was talking to him, too. I knew I would be in trouble because…guess what. I was still on probation for stealing from the university. There I sat, wishing I could disappear.

The next business day, I went to see my state probation officer, and he told me that he would wait until my court date before he revoked my probation.

I went on with life while I waited for my court day, and then, it happened. Four months after the DUI, Rico Suave did not pick up our son at his scheduled time. I had drunk a few Bud Ices, the ones in the tall can, and I'd put our son in the car. I headed to set the record straight because he had not paid the daycare, bought any Pampers, and had not shown up to pick up our son. I am grateful that the grace of God was with me and my son. My oldest son had a basketball game in Atlanta and needed me to be there with him. I needed to be in Atlanta and was frustrated and angry. Now, this is no excuse for my behavior. I am simply telling you the truth of the story. I am revealing this so that you or those you know will understand that, sometimes, we make crazy decisions and choices. I am telling this truth because I know that someone needs to know that even in your chaos and poor decision making, God's grace is still sufficient.

Well, when I arrived at Rico Suave's house, he was booed up. The girl was lying across the bed like Lola Filano, and he was out back. I was so angry with him, and I will be the first to say my Bud Ice and I acted like complete fools. Rico Suave and I fought, and it got ugly. I was angry, hurt, belligerent, and was a self-made fool. Remember, he came in as a cheater. But in my brokenness, I wanted what I wanted, and I got a big bag of brokenness and heartache.

That day was the last day that I contended with being a fool. A self-made fool was still a fool. I was not proud of my actions on that day. I spat in his face! Of course, he hit me back. I took my car and put it in drive and drove it directly into his car. I left the scene, came back, and drove into his car again. I, then, jumped out and took my keys and keyed his car with all that I had. I honestly think those marks are still on his truck. His girlfriend held our son on her hip as if she had won a prize.

I, then, drove off and headed to Atlanta to the basketball tournament like I was supposed to. God's grace was so sufficient, and I know, for a fact, that God drove the car. I called my best friends and my pastor and kept it moving. My ex and his female friend called the police and made a very thorough report; some things were true, and others were fabricated.

I knew I would have to turn myself in to the authorities for what I had done, so that night, I went to Rockdale Hospital and checked myself in while he, his girlfriend, and our son went to the park. When I look back, I needed the rest. I needed to calm my emotions. My dear friend Felecia stayed with me at the hospital until they sent me to Georgia Regional for a day or two of rest.

When I came home, I knew I would have to answer to the warrant for going over to his house and acting a fool. My pastor at the time was Pastor Nathan Durham. That man walked me through that stuff like a champ, and I could never thank him and his wife enough. He called the sheriff's department and let them know that I would be turning myself in, and the sheriff promised him that I would be out before the weekend started. Needless to say, I was out. However, I had to contend with (you guessed it) my probation officer.

Tavis C. Taylor

This time, I had a different officer, and he said, "You have two cases, not one, Ms. Taylor, and honestly, if you are found guilty on either charge, I am going to have to send you back to prison."

The officer was within his job duties and legal rights to send me back to prison for violating my probation. I was on a path of self-destruction, and I was headed there fast.

That happened in 2010, and my court date did not come up until January 2011.

Looking for Trouble

In January 2011, I needed a break. Waiting for the two court dates sent me spiraling into depression. It was so bad that I had programmed myself to be depressed only when the boys were at school. One weekend, I spent the night with my best friend Mattie, who was one of the greatest hostesses, so I was able to relax and refresh my thinking. One Monday morning, I received a call from my attorney. He informed me that I was supposed to be in court for the DUI. I had not received a call or message from his officer. Needless to say, that did not matter. I was supposed to be in court. He was able to ask the judge to allow me to show up on that Wednesday, and by that time, I was to be prepared to serve thirteen days in the Gwinnett County jail for my second DUI. I almost lost my mind. Wait! I'm going to have to leave my boys again? I needed help and the type of help I needed was bigger than a drink!

I spoke to my parents and studied myself as I prepared for jail again. My family kept my boys. When I entered the facility for my stay, I honestly thought I would lose my mind. I needed answers. I wanted to know what I could do differently and how. Church, as usual, was not doing it. I needed more. I needed a deliverance from ME.

While serving time at the Gwinnett County jail (Now remember, I was doing jail ministry at the Fulton County jail.), I prayed again. I asked God to show me in the Bible where He used other people who had messed up really bad. He showed me, and I started writing my first book while incarcerated.

As my days were narrowing down, I became fearful. They called my name and told me it was time to go. I was walking out, and one of the two guards called my name. "TAVIS!" she screamed as she looked down at the computer system. "TAVIS TAYLOR!" I paused with fear because I thought she was calling me back. When you are on probation and you violate your probation, they will put a hold on you and make you go to court. Once you are in court, you explain what you did to be arrested and why. When this happens, the probation officer typically makes you sit in jail for approximately thirty days. Y'all, I didn't have thirty days to give. Nevertheless, the other officer screamed, "Leave that lady alone." I continued walking out the door and literally fell to my knees as my best friend picked me up to take me home. I cried all the way home because this experience nearly broke me.

While I was grateful that they did not put a hold in the system because of my probation violation, on the next business day, I would have to go see my probation officer! Remember, the probation officer told me he would violate the probation that I was on and I would go back to prison.

The dreaded day came, and I walked into the state probation office and faced my fear again. As I sat down, I told him where I had been. Then, he looked at me and said, "I am not sure why I am doing this, but I am going to let you go. When you go to court for your case against your son's father, if you plead guilty, I must have you serve time."

I said, "Yes, sir."

I ran out and cried, thanking God for my freedom. I thanked God for freeing me in the midst of my chaos. It was by the grace of God that I was set free.

Tavis C. Taylor

Rededicated

While serving time in the Gwinnett County jail, I became overly frustrated with me! I was angry that I was yet again in a place of darkness and despair. To make matters worse, I was a regular minister at the Fulton County jail. I had been ministering to the women there since my release in 2004, and here I sat in their very same seat again. I honestly didn't know why I kept making less than favorable decisions in my life.

I asked God to reveal Himself to me. All I had was a Bible to read, and honestly, that was more than enough. I could feel that my life was not over, that God would still use me. So I asked Him to show me in the Bible where He had used people who constantly made mistakes. I began to read the word of God, and the revelation was like never before. The stories looked different because they were different, and they sounded different. Moses, Paul, and David became my heroes, and I was able to trust that my life was not over and that God would and could still use me, so I started writing. I talked to different inmates and literally polled them on different aspects of incarceration while I was there. Needless to say, my first book, *Behind the Walls: Making it Through a Tough Time*, was born. It was written and published in less than two months. This book is on Amazon. Below is the write up for that particular work:

The cold bars of prison did not stop one woman from finding the light amid the darkness. With her newly released book, *Behind the Walls: Making it Through a Tough Time*, author Tavis Taylor shares this hope, not only with inmates, but with others who feel like they are trapped in their own cell. "Most inmates are really scared and feel alone during their incarceration process. Some want to pray, but just don't know how. This book can assist in the growth process as far as your relationship with God is concerned," Taylor shares. The groundbreaking message in this book will open the reader's eyes to the truth about getting into, staying, and being productive in the body of Christ. It helps one deal with questions and concerns about getting close to God while being incarcerated. It shows how to utilize scripture for prayer as well. But most of all, it assists individuals in releasing the guilt on the sin committed to better move forward while incarcerated. Ultimately, it leaves messages that are aimed to be treasured upon one's freedom. Part journal and part self-help, *Behind the Walls* was tailored to shed light on some of life's darkest concerns. With thought-

Tavis C. Taylor

provoking Biblical scriptures and eye-opening personal reflections, this book will bring comfort to the heart and motivation to the spirit.

This book was birthed out of my own personal pain and chaos. It is full of experiences and information that can help those who are incarcerated and those who have family members or friends who are incarcerated. I made yet another commitment to God to continue to do the work that He had called me to do.

Answering the Call

Upon my release, I continued my work to help women who were incarcerated. Since 2004, I have ministered consistently at the Fulton County jail. The ministry has included teaching anger management, parenting, life skills, GED, and speaking to the women. My ministry, Behind the Walls Ministries, has donated over 1,000 copies of my book, *Behind the Wall: Making It through a Tough Time*, to those who are incarcerated. It blesses me to go in and minister, and it also blesses me to receive letters from those who have read my book and write to say how the book has impacted their lives. Since then, I have also developed a relationship with the Clarke County jail, and there are books in that jail as well. My jail ministry was birthed out of a place of pain for me.

Tavis C. Taylor

A Turning Point

The year 2012 was one of the worst years of my life. I wanted to give up, but my strength was built on my pain. I knew that, if I could make it, I could encourage others to do the same. I honestly didn't want to die in my pain, and I didn't want others to die in theirs. I was in church. I was a minister, and I was walking around, wondering why others did not see my pain. I resolved that, if I was stuck behind walls of physical, mental, and emotional prisons, then I knew I was not the only one. I knew that others needed to know the true power of God and His forgiveness. I knew I needed to tell my story and tell others that they could make it. I didn't want to leave the world without being used by God. After all of that, I re-surrendered. I re-surrendered to the process and power of God again.

I was tired of going in circles and cycles of defeat and despair. I was in a pit of despair when God sent an apostle into my life to pass me a note. I never knew anything about being called by God to save a nation or a people. I never knew that the enemy was real. I never knew that there was a chance that, from birth, the devil had been trying to kill me. The note that was passed along that day changed the trajectory of my life and my thought patterns. I began to investigate the different spirits and warfare.

When I was growing up, I knew I was different, but I had no idea what being chosen and called really meant. I even made an attempt at attending a seminary, but I did not receive answers there. As a matter of fact, that idea went out the window on the first day of seminary. There was a symposium that day, and the first person I saw was a well-known pastor who was a friend of my pastor. The reason I was floored was because, instead of counseling me, he tried to sleep with me. So That was an epic fail as well.

Tavis C. Taylor

Cold Winter & Summer Heat

But there was still the other case. I was so tired! The case with my son's father had been decided the previous year, and I had not been summoned to court as of January. You won't believe this, but three days after I came home from the thirteen-day stay for my second DUI, the letter to attend court for acting a fool at my son's father's house came in the mail. I could not breathe. I could not focus. This was too much.

I called my attorney and learned he was reluctant to take my case because he didn't want me to waste my money if my probation officer was going to arrest me. He talked about how some attorneys took their clients' money when they knew there was a chance of their probation being violated.

My date in court came, and I wasn't ready. I wasn't ready for what I'd read in the police report, and I wasn't ready for what was next.

After reading the report and talking to my attorney, I pled guilty to the charges. Because I'd fought in public and in front of my son, I was charged with, luckily, only a misdemeanor and not a felony.

After court, I had to go and see the same probation officer who had made it very clear that I was going to prison for violating my probation. So I trekked in there, and I plopped down in the chair. I told him about what happened in court, and then he said, "Ms. Taylor, if I let you go, will you please stay out of trouble?'

I said, "Yes, sir."

I left there victorious, yet depleted. I was tired but relieved that all my legal issues were over. At least, I thought they were.

I left the probation office feeling a sense of relief. I knew then I had been given yet another chance by God. I left there, went home, and embraced my sons. I cried all night, wondering what was wrong with me. I was wondering why I could not get it right. I prayed to God, asking Him to change me, but nothing was happening. I was in church and doing what I thought God wanted me to do, but my life was still a total wreck. At this point, I was still in love with my younger son's father, and we were still going back and forth, having relations. I decided that I should focus on myself and my children as well, and he decided he was going to focus on himself, so we stopped having relations; instead, we just co-parented our son.

Probation, Violation, and Grace

With all that had taken place, I now had to contend with being on probation for three offenses. I had three different probation officers to report to at three different times each month. My license was suspended for two years, and I would have to have an interlock (blow machine) in my car.

While on all three probations, I earnestly looked for gainful employment, and in 2012, I landed a job working as an administrative assistant in a tax office. This was part-time work, and I made $8 per hour during tax season and $600 per month in the off-season. I was honestly glad to be out of trouble and just grateful to be free.

So each month, I had to trek to see each of my probation officers. Yep, all three of them. When I saw them, I had to either have a payment in my hand or have mailed a payment in. At some point during this time, I had enrolled in seminary, in hopes that, by studying about God and learning how faith actually worked, I would be okay.

I would play musical chairs with the payments to the probation officers. I was responsible for reporting to three different locations for probation, one in Gwinnett County and two in Monroe, Georgia.

The Gwinnett probation officer was the officer responsible for supervising my second DUI. She was nice but threatened to take me back to court because I had paid all of the fine but $64. During this probation, I had to put the interlock system in my car. This was a system that I had to blow in when I got in and out of my car. In order to drive anywhere, that system had to be in my car. I had the system installed, and my car had to sit for a few days. The problem was, from the time of my arrest until the time I had the device installed, the laws changed, and I had to get permission from the judge to install the device. All these mistakes cost me mentally and financially. The irony of all of this chaos was that it all cost a great deal of money. Each probation required a payment. The interlock system required a payment, and even breathing required a payment. I was burned out financially and emotionally.

After getting the device installed, I was able to go to the DMV and obtain my provisional driver's license. Until then, I'd had to depend on family and friends to take me and my children places.

Tavis C. Taylor

Driving with my children became an art. I hid the system under the seat as best as I could and would make sure I timed when I had to blow in the system so that I would not embarrass my boys.

In December of 2012, I had to go back to court twice in the same week. On that Tuesday, I went to child support court.

Back to Lock Up: Take One

I'm not sure why these roller-coaster rides were taking place. At this point, I was walking the straight and narrow. I had made peace with my past and was trying to be a law-abiding citizen.

Remember the nice state probation officer? He quit in 2013, and I was assigned to see the supervisor at the Monroe location. When I went in, he yelled at me, telling me that I owed so much money. He told me that he would have to call Fulton County, and I should call him the next day. I spent the next few days calling him, to no avail. Do you remember the story at the beginning of the book? This is where that story started. When I went in for my monthly visit, I was told to sit down and wait. Now I had been calling this man for two weeks, and he never returned my calls. When I went in to visit, he had a warrant issued for my arrest for failure to pay my fine completely off. The issue was, he did not read my paperwork. My sentence was a consecutive sentence, meaning I would serve one sentence of ten years, and then, I had another sentence of ten years on probation to pay the restitution for the money that I stole. He did not read the paperwork correctly and thought I should go to jail for not paying enough of the money back.

The state probation officer called me back and asked me a few questions. After answering her line of questioning, she then told me that she would be arresting me. She allowed me to call my sisters and tell them. What was crazy was, that morning, I had gone to the DMV to get my driver's license after not having one for two years. I was not quite sure why this warrant did not show up, but it didn't.

I went to jail that day, thus the opening of the book. Remember, they let me go. That release happened so fast.

I was looking crazy because I had not been there long. At least, not long enough for a deputy to drive from the Fulton County jail to the Walton County jail to pick me up. Let me explain, in 2001, my case originated in Fulton County; therefore, anything that happened to me in any other county would mean that Fulton County would have to come and pick me up, take me to jail, and I would eventually go to court. Then, I thought, Wow! They really wanted me bad because they got here so quick. So I looked at the jailer and asked the daunting question, "Is Fulton County here to get me?"

"No," she said, looking puzzled. "We called Fulton County, and they told us to let you go."

As we were walking, she informed me that I would be free to go and I could use their telephone to call someone. I asked for the phone, and then it hit me, "You are free, Tavis. Just go." And go I did. I walked out and ran as fast as I could to a friend's house who did not live far from there. I asked her to give me a ride to my grandmother's house (Remember, the town I am from is very small). In the meantime, I used her telephone to call my supervisor at the time, who just so happened to be talking to my youngest sister on the telephone. My flight to freedom happened so fast that, when my supervisor heard me say, "Hello" from a mutual friend's telephone, she immediately thought I had made a dramatic jailbreak. No, I am not kidding. Her response was, "No, T! Go back!" After I informed her that I was free, she was relieved. However, I knew I had to contend with whatever had just taken place concerning my arrest. And that, my dear, was the beginning of the ending of a web that I had spun that, honestly, seemed as if it was never going to end. When I left the jail, I knew I would have to call the jail to get clarity on what happened.

One of my friends' sisters worked at the Fulton County jail and answered the call when it came in. She later informed me that she knew what I was doing and how I was working for God. She was relieving a co-worker for lunch when the call came in, and she was the one who

Tavis C. Taylor

told them to let me go! She informed me that I needed to call my probation officer the next day. I called the Walton County jail and spoke to one of the lieutenants that I knew by name. Her response was, "Tavis, this is a live warrant. Make sure you call your officer tomorrow. We should not have let you go." My heart immediately sank to the pit of my stomach. This meant that there was an active warrant for my arrest that I needed to take care of. That night was a long night. I had visions of the police coming to my house, kicking my door down and arresting me. I finally fell asleep and was awakened by my alarm clock. This alarm was set for me to wake my children up and prepare them for school. However, on this morning, it had an additional meaning. It meant I would have to drop my sons off at school and investigate the warrant from the previous day.

The next day, I went to my office and called the officer. And he hostilely said to me, "Ms. Taylor, you need to go to Fulton County now and turn yourself in."

I burst into tears and started screaming, "No, no, not again! What about my children?" By that time, my supervisor had come in and was listening. The officer told me to send him $1,500 by a certain time that day, and he would allow me to be a "walk-in" probation violator, meaning I would not have to go to jail, but I would have to go to court. My supervisor at the time loaned me the money, and my best friend took the money to them. My court date was set. Two weeks later, I walked into the Fulton County jail to court.

What I immediately noticed was that I was the only person who was on that side of the glass. I was seated in the area where the family came to court. I looked around and counted fifty-two people in jail uniforms who had violated their probations. The judge gave us all a speech: "You have wasted thirty days of your life being in jail." All I could think was, Wait! I am the only one on this side of the glass. Thank you, Lord! After seeing the hand of the Lord, I started believing differently.

After God did that, I vowed that I would obey God and the promise to go back into the jail and honor my vow to preach the gospel in jails.

So I went to the Fulton County jail to update my ID so that I could go in and minister and teach. As I was sitting there, I saw several people walk by, looking crazy. This fine, bald-headed Caucasian man came out and asked about me. Now, my crazy behind thought he was trying to hit on me because I thought I was looking cute. When I went in, he rolled a chair close to my face and asked me about several people in my case. "Do you know this person and that person?" he said. "We have a warrant for your arrest." The issue was, they had called downtown for the warrant and the lady had forgotten to fax it. She went to lunch. But God was so faithful.

My friend's sister who answered the phone before was at the office relieving the lady for lunch, and she had answered the phone. I could hear her yelling in the phone. Do you remember when I went in and answered the warrant as a walk-in? Well, they forgot to take the warrant out of the system! They were prepared to arrest me on that day! After speaking to the officer, she told me that they were going to arrest me the day that she called me to come and get my ID for volunteering. She thought the warrant was active, and they just wanted to get me off the street.

God is so amazing because, when they called me to come in for my ID, I called the counselor who was the director of the New Beginnings Program at the Fulton County jail, but he was not there. I decided to wait for him before I went in to get my ID. They called again, and I was unavailable. The irony of it was I think God was trying to warn me about what would happen. I thought about the fact that she had called for me to come and get my volunteer ID, and I asked the daunting question, "So if I would have come here before, would you have locked me up?"

She said, "Yes, and you better be glad you didn't come last week because the lady who relieved me while I was on vacation would have arrested you first and asked questions later."

As the officer was preparing my ID, I politely informed her that I would never return, and I would never volunteer at any jail another day in my life.

When I left there, I had several messages from the young lady who worked for the county. She was trying to warn me that they were trying to arrest me. She told her sister, "I don't know what God has in store for Tavis to do, but the devil is trying to stop it."

That day took a toll on me, and I waited months before I went back in to volunteer. The program and jail ministry were such great passions of mine because jail is such a place of confusion, darkness, hopelessness, and despair. I loved going back in and telling my story because, if God can open jail doors for me, He can do it for anyone.

The number of times that God spared me simply because of His grace is too numerous to count. I am sharing this story in hopes that, sure as Jesus is Lord, someone will get the strength to begin again. My hope is that you will no longer walk around in a world of guilt because of your actions.

This doesn't end my story. There is still more to tell. What I will tell you is that, with every bad decision, with every bit of self-created chaos, I realized how much I needed deliverance and counseling. I understand that some will read this and never understand my chaos. However, this entire story, my story, is for those who have truly messed up. It is for those who need a modern-day story about miracles. There are quite a few scriptures that I love that I lean on. The Lord was with me during every dumb and stupid decision that I made. I am so grateful that God did not leave me.

So I was over the penal system, justice system, and baby daddies. I just wanted to raise my children, and that was it. After all this chaos, my life became more consistent, and the penal system was no longer a threat to me, nor I to it.

I started attending heavy counseling in 2013, and since then, I have undergone several deliverance sessions so that my old demons would no longer take root in my life. I have since published several books. I am a certified Christian counselor, parent blogger, and administrator by trade. My journey has allowed me to speak into the lives of others, giving them hope against hope. I enjoy encouraging those who have fought to survive traumatic situations in their lives. My son's father and I co-parent amicably, and I am grateful to God for that.

Building a Business and a Brand

Being an entrepreneur was never a dream of mine. I always wanted to be a lawyer or a professor. If those didn't work, I honestly didn't know what I would do. As I grew older, administrative work became my field of choice, and that is the field I worked in prior to all of this chaos.

After making some of the decisions I made, I realized that working a normal nine-to-five job would not be an option. However, I needed to make a living for my children and myself. Of course, I applied to jobs and careers, but my background check would cause me to become disqualified after the different human resource representatives ran this standard check.

Therefore, building a business and a brand was an easy decision from that perspective. I knew that I would be ridiculed by those who knew some or parts of my story because people tend to hold you hostage by what they know or what they've heard. However, I had to make a choice. Either I stayed where I was and allowed all my skills and experience to die, or I could truly trust the word of God and that

God had forgiven me and that God was a God of second chances. I knew people would talk, but going through what I had went through built my public-ridicule muscle up, and I could move forward. I pressed through the conversations, the comments, and the shunning that took place. I pressed through people calling people and telling them not to work with me or not to trust me. I pressed through people not supporting me, not sharing my work, not hiring me, and not even buying a book. I even pressed through people taking my ideas and making them their own.

At that point, it wasn't about what was outside of me. It was about what I believed to be true on the inside.

Facing the Past

There is not a day that goes by that I am not reminded of my years of chaos and bad decision making. It shows up when I apply for contracts. It visits me when I want to travel. It also shows up when applying for jobs.

I have decided to make the most of it by telling my story. I tell others that they can overcome because I overcame. I share my stories because it is my goal to be a beacon of hope for someone who wants to give up.

The mistakes that I made in the past forced me to constantly stare my past decisions directly in the face. And in doing so, I have decided to look at those mistakes from a place of victory, instead of victimization. I chose to face the past from a place of "Look what God has brought me through," instead of "I can't believe I did that." This affords me the opportunity to bask in God's grace and His mercy. This affords me the opportunity to understand that God loves me so much that, even in my personal chaos, He is still God. He is sovereign, and

Tavis C. Taylor

He truly can use whomever He chooses. I am simply grateful that He has chosen me. Therefore, I choose to tell my past as a testimony of being an overcomer with the understanding that we overcome by the blood of the lamb and the word of our testimony.

Graced to Forgive

First things first, I honestly believe that there is power in forgiveness and in forgiving others, and there is a superpower in forgiving yourself. I had to realize that, yes, I was powerful and worthy of self-forgiveness simply because God tells us not to hold ourselves in guilt and condemnation. Yes, I had to forgive my perpetrators, but the one person that I had to ultimately forgive was myself. I had to realize that my value and self-worth would never appear if I did not understand that the condemnation, guilt, and shame that I had allowed to consume me was not serving a purpose. Instead, I chose to forgive myself, hold my head up, and walk uprightly because of who I am in Christ Jesus.

I had spent so much time equating my value, or lack thereof, with my mistakes. I allowed what others thought and said for years to consume my thoughts and internally define who I was. But I had to move past that. I had to move past any social conditioning and internal conditioning and allow the word of God to set me free. It was at that point that I realized that God had given me the grace to forgive myself and others. That is the grace and boldness that others see in my personality today. After all, it is by the grace of God that I am able to walk with my head up high after I spent years making embarrassing, shameful decisions and mistakes.

Epilogue: Looking Ahead

As I look ahead at what life offers and what God has called me to do, I will continue to tell my testimony and my story. I will continue to share the goodness of God with those God sends my way. I am now clear that my life is a gift and a testimony for the kingdom. It is a story to be shared to help others.

My story is a story of chaos and confusion, but it is also a story of tests, trials, and triumphs. Taking the "Scenic Route to Purpose" has been draining yet rewarding. I hope, by telling my story, others will know that nothing they have been through will be wasted if they allow God to truly use their story. In addition, I truly pray that the readers of this book whether these stories are relatable to you or someone you know, realize that "And we know that all things work together for good to them that love God, to them who are called according to his purpose" (Romans 8:28 KJV).

Tavis C. Taylor

Acknowledgements

A special thank you to God, Jesus, and Holy Spirit.

My two little brown boys, Tyler and Adrian

Mom & Dad

The Lees

Prayer warriors throughout the years

All of current prayer warriors and E. Danielle Butler for not giving
up on this project.

The Scenic Route to Purpose

Tavis C. Taylor

About the Author

Tavis C. Taylor is a passionate Minister, Author, and Motivational Speaker who has quickly earned the reputation as an ambassador of positive thinking and compassionate leader. Widely known for her personable, consultative, and down-to-earth approach, her inspirational work—both in written and spoken form—has an immediate transformative ripple effect on each and every participant and reader. Above all, she instills people with the tools they need to alter their perceptions and completely change their lives.

Currently, Tavis serves as the Founder of Behind the Walls Ministries. She is also the author of *Behind the Walls: Making it Through a Tough Time*. With these two empowering ventures, she is on a mission to liberate people from the financial, emotional, or mental walls that they have created for themselves. Ultimately, her unwavering faith in God and her first-hand experiences paved her career path and turned her passion for helping others into her one true calling.

Tavis holds a Bachelor of Science degree in Hospitality Administration and a Master's degree in Public Administration from Georgia State University. She has earned her Christian Counselor Certification and is also Certified Anger Management Specialist II.

Tavis C. Taylor

Other Books by Tavis Taylor

Behind the Walls: Making it Through a Tough Time

Parenting Ain't for Punks

Help! My Teen is Driving Me Crazy

Praying it Forward: A 21 Day Guide to Fasting and Praying for Your Children

Made in the USA
Columbia, SC
25 September 2020